What My Father Believed

What

My

Poems by Robert Wrigley

Father

Believed

University of Illinois Press : Urbana and Chicago

Publication of this work was supported in part by grants from the National Endowment for the Arts and the Illinois Arts Council, a state agency.

Manufactured in the United States of America

P 5 4 3 2 1

This book is printed on acid-free paper.

Some of the poems in this book have appeared previously in the following publications:

CutBank: Steelhead
The Georgia Review: Economics
The Gettysburg Reveiw: Ravens at Deer Creek
The Iowa Review: Parking
The Kenyon Review: Sinatra
The Missouri Review: The Big Dipper
New England Review & Bread Loaf Quarterly: The Wishing Tree
The New Virginia Review: The Overcoat; The Scar; The White Cat
Northern Lights: His Father's Whistle
The Pacific Review: In the Dark Pool, Finding You
Palouse Journal: Onions
Poetry: American Manhood; Camping; C.O.; For the Last Summer;
    What My Father Believed
Poetry Northwest: Dust; The Grandmothers
Shenandoah: Body and Soul; Night Calls; Night Rising; Shrapnel
Virginia Quarterly Review: Invisible Men
Witness: Light after Light
Yellow Silk: Flight

"Flight" and "In the Dark Pool, Finding You" also appeared in *In the Dark Pool,* a chapbook published by Confluence Press in 1987.

Library of Congress Cataloging-in-Publication Data

Wrigley, Robert, 1951–
    What my father believed : poems / by Robert Wrigley.
        p.   cm.
    ISBN 0-252-06168-3 (pb.)
    I. Title.
    PS3573.R58W47   1991
    811'.54—dc20   90-41290
                                                            CIP

for my father & for my children

Contents

Logic and sermons never convince,
The damp of the night drives deeper into my soul.

—Whitman

American Manhood

In the dull ache that is midnight for a boy
his age, I heard the sound of him first:
hiss of the pistol-grip hose from the garden
and the clatter a watery arc makes
coming down silver under streetlights,
on the day-warmed pavement of the road.
And though I muttered at first
to be awakened, I stand now in the window
upstairs, naked and alert, the cool breeze
sweet with the blossoms of locusts.

My wife murmurs, stirs. She is a slope of white
in the bedclothes, dunes of softness
below the light from the window
and the single blind eye of the clock.
"It's just Travis," I say, hoping
she'll lapse again into sleep.

I hope she'll sleep because he is a boy,
fourteen, soft yet himself, unwhiskered.
He believes he is the only one
awake, the only one alive in a world
of cruel nights and unbearable silence.
His parents snore, their house is dark.
He crouches on the curb
in just his pajama bottoms, barefoot,
swirling figure eights into the air trafficked
by insects and the fluttering, hunting bats.

Tonight he speaks a language I believe
I must have known, in the time before, those years
when a boy's body imagines the world, the heartbeat
rhythm of water on the road, the riches

coined by streetlights, the smell of the night
that is everything at once, alterable
and contained—all that keeps him awake
long after I've gone back to bed.

But before sleep comes, I listen, until the noise
he makes is my own even breathing, and I remember how
the old rented guitar I learned on smelled of music,
how the young married woman across the street
robbed me of the power of speech,
and how I wandered one night the alleys
of the town I grew up in, a brick in my hand,
breaking thermometers, taillights, and windows,
and went home and laughed aloud and wept.

Night Rising

After an hour of fighting it, I pull
on my boots, leave my son sleeping
in the tent, and stand pissing in a darkness
absolute to my burning, sleep-swollen eyes.
In the last year this rising has become
common, a nightly battle of will and bodily want,
the fist and the clamped thighs, the dark.

A day of steady rain, fog in the bones,
bad fishing, has left me halfway through the night
sore from sleeping on the ground. I chill
as my bladder empties. From the great dying
cedars droplets fall on my bare back and arms,
the river murmurs in the distance.
Before I awakened, at the dim edge of urgency,
I dreamed my own father groaning in the night,
easing from the door of the station wagon
we slept in, the cool heft of night air
hitting me, the dome light momentarily on,
then off, on again, then off for good.

Now groggy with sleep, I can't recall
what is memory and what is dream.
If such a night ever happened—the minute
of solitary half-sleep, darkness tattooed
with the dome light's blue afterimages—
I can't say. Nor can I say for sure when I finish
which way I've come from the tent.

Without moon or stars or flashlight, I listen
behind the river for rain, the ping of it
on a left-out pot, drum on the pickup's hood.
I consider calling my son's name

but know how soundly the boy sleeps,
how the bellow it would take to wake him
would frighten him as well. So I move,
one slow step after another, my hands
swimming the black fog before me,
finding my way in time.

His Father's Whistle

For hours the boy fought sleep,
strained against the whir of cicadas, moths
at the screens bumbling, night's
silver breezes, to hear out on the country road
his father's car rumbling in gravel.
He watched for the sweep of headlights
on the ceiling, a quick rush down
the driveway, then footsteps barely audible
over the lawn, his father's whistle.
Half a verse, a sliver of chorus, and his father was in
the house, quiet, the boy already drifting
in the night, asleep before the hand caressed his face.

It seemed to the boy that his life would be this way
forever, that out of the murmuring shadows,
the terror of distance, the danger of all
he did not know, there would come an order
like the one a melody imposed upon silence,
his father's whistle among night sounds,
as though breath, a song,
and a boy's simple fear of the dark,
were a man's only reasons for whistling.

Economics

He learned economics in the shade
of a truck, a flatbed owned by the man
he worked for, who owned as well the tons
of concrete on it, owned the farm never farmed
but mowed, the Ford dealership in town,
a great white house across the way, and a daughter
there with her friends, sunbathing by the pool.
A ton of cement in hundred-pound bags
he'd already stacked on pallets in the barn.
It was Saturday, after lunch, sun seared
his neck and shoulders, flickered
from the drops on the girls by the pool,
and shone in the suffocating dust
he saw through. Though his eyes were closed
when the kick hit his heels,
he wasn't sleeping. He was awake
and dreaming in the splashes and laughter,
resting in the dust and truck-smelling shade,
leaned against a gritty rear wheel.

And so it was the joy he imagined
tied then to the owner's sneer
and warning. Joy, and the rage he let build
through a ton-and-a-half of lifting
and lugging, the loathing for a man
who owned all the world he could see
from high on the back of a flatbed truck,
sweeping dust into the air
and watching when that man came out
to the pool, soft and flabby,
and grinned through an oafish cannonball
that made the girls laugh, applauding like seals.
It was a rage that cooked in his old

black car, that ground in its slow start,
and lunged like its badly slipping clutch.
He longed in his sweat for speed and oblivion,
the thrum of good tires, the deep-lunged roar
of power, a wheel in his hands
like a weapon, turn by premeditated turn.

"You best work, boy, or your whole life'll be
as shitty as today." When the kick had come
he flinched, involuntarily. His one knee rose,
his left arm blocked his face, and in the grit
of his right glove his fist closed on
the readiness to hit. He was ashamed
to be caught, ashamed for his flinch,
ashamed he could not, as the owner glared down
at his startled eyes, leap to his feet and murder him.
He was ashamed by his silence, by the ache
even then in his back and arms, the guilt
he could never disprove. The route home
that day derided him, maddeningly slow
through marginal farms and identical suburbs.
His mother's howdy-doo repulsed him,
and his father's little wink seemed the grimace
of a ninny. It was Saturday night,
he had no date, but didn't sleep until morning,
when he rose anyway, hating his face in the mirror.

Monday, washing as always the endless line
of new cars, he began to understand
the limitations of revenge: murder, fire,
the daughter's humiliation at school—
these were risks he couldn't take. Even scratches
here and there on the cars. He cursed his luck
and scrubbed, twisted the chamois so tightly
it tore, and Sven, the old one-armed Swede

he worked with, shook his head and sighed.
"You just wash, Hercules," he said. "I'll dry 'em."
So he went on, lathering and scrubbing,
quiet, Sven telling dirty jokes,
analyzing the bouquet, the savor of women,
offering his wisdom in every field
until the boy threw down his sponge, spit,
looked the old man deeply in the eye
and asked him in all his feeble goddam brilliance
what the hell was he doing here, washing cars
a half a buck a crack with a boy.

And when he saw Sven's expression
it almost came out, all the simple story
about sweat and mistakes, cement and rage
and the long ride to nowhere through a life
he couldn't stand. What would it have taken
for the shame to come out, the shame
now for hurting an old man, for kicking,
like any cool and flabby man who owned a world.
Instead the boy worked, behind him
Sven mopping up, silent until the last three sedans,
when he flipped the chamois on a hood and said,
"Here, goddam ye. I'm tired. You finish 'em."
And so he was alone at the end,
when the owner's daughter arrived, brown
and gut-hurtingly beautiful in a shiny new car.
She waved to him and smiled, Sven was gone,
his blood sped in his veins, and he knew
she'd come no nearer to him ever in his life.

For the Last Summer

That summer with a thousand Julys
nothing mattered but the sweat on a girl's chest,
the sun's crazy blue weather, and a young man's
hands electric with want. The wind
above convertibles sighed in the cottonwood leaves,
the stars were stars, and the moon ached
in its own silver heaven. He was king
of the swath a train whistle cut.

Crazy for speed, he held the girl and the wheel
and plummeted toward the bottomlands,
foundry lights ablaze in the distance,
and war let him sing the songs he swore
he'd never forget. That summer
of week-long nights, blossom-dark,
fragrant with dew and a dust
as fine as milled flour, he dreamed.

And his dreams were all glory and light,
line drives that never fell, his friends
his friends forever, and war
let him sleep until noon and wake
with the scent of his girl around him,
remembering the night before—
how he sang of a loss he couldn't imagine,
of broken hearts he could almost believe.

That summer with a thousand Julys
the sun going down each afternoon was more
beautiful than the day before, the factory smoke
vermilion and rust in its slant, and the night-
hawks like needles stitching the darkness down.

Nothing smelled as sweet as the gasoline
he pumped, nothing arced so cleanly
as the shop towels he tossed toward their baskets.

The world rode shotgun and reclined
on the seat of his car, lovely in the glow
from the dash lights, soft and warm.
and he knew what it meant to adore. War
let him dawdle there, virtuoso of the radio,
king of the push buttons, and all that played
for him, in the only hours of his life he ever knew
as his own, was music, music, music.

Sinatra

That skinny fuck-up, all recklessness and bones,
the one my father called feisty, was Prewitt
in the movie, and in my twelve-year-old conception
of things, in the magical drive-in dark, I knew it
was true: I'd found the man I'd aim to be.
Suddenly, the fact that I could sing meant something,
and one long day of rain my father let me
ease from their even rows his dazzling
collection of records. Among the heavy seventy-eights
of Gershwin and Lanza, I found him there—
Sinatra in a rumpled suit, hands in his pockets, hate
in his eyes, or love, I couldn't tell. He peered
off the jacket with steel in his blood, with style,
while every song was love gone wrong, old tunes
blue with heartbreak. I believed his smile
was deadly, that weakness was ruin.
Five years later, still not disabused
of the cinemascope hokum, it was Sinatra, not me,
flipping off the nightclub bouncer, the fake ID I'd used
slipped neatly into the till. And tonight, twenty
years further into our lives, Sinatra and I have both outlived
those early days. The drive-ins are gone, and Gaslight Square,
and that bouncer, who grinned and shoved
me twice, out the door and against the front wall,
and hit me once so hard in the gut
that I knelt among the sidewalk crowd and cried, all
the night's easy beers boiling out.
There are whole weeks now
when I'm trapped inside the stereo's thrall,
when the old Sinatra convincingly sings how
love goes wrong. A little light turns the walls

golden, I have solitaire and sentiment, whiskey and comfort,
but I wake up empty. Daydreams run
my life now, and I wonder what sort
of man I might've been, what sort I've become.

The Flight Line

Summer days that paved world shimmers with heat,
and my father walking the flight line to his car
might be imaginary, a mirage, the wavery light
fluttering his clothes like silks. Behind him
fighters scream far out of proportion
to their size and distance, and the transports
—huge as buildings—rock the earth
as they lumber barely aloft.

It is 1969. After the long drive home
he falls asleep in his chair, the newspaper unfolding
over his lap and legs, ears ringing
in the unreliable silence. He is already half-deaf,
but I want him to hear my rants against the war
his planes are bound for.

Over dinner the tv's roar keeps us quiet.
At right angles to each other
my father and I fume with rage,
my mother and sister tense as cats.
This is how we live the year before I'm drafted,
suffering ourselves and the pretense of meals,
until one night, when the weekly dead are known,
and we are caught, frozen, peering
into the tablecloth's cheerful pattern,
listening against our will to the newsman.
On that night, as on so many others,
I cannot contain myself and lift my eyes and see
my mother, her head bowed, stirring absently at her food,
and then begin the turn toward my father,
prepared again to say what I should not,
to say it and mean it, to spill it out
like bile on the table before us—
my hatred for the nation of my birth.

But this night, when I turn to him
I say nothing. Slowly his head shakes
side to side, his face blank as wind,
and I am so stunned to see him crying
I can say nothing at all
before he is up and leaving the table,
and we are alone with the televised war.

On the screen in black and white, soldiers
my own age speak and grin and bleed.
It is an enormous distance across that room, that house
in the American heartland, miles from the planes,
the shimmering image of the flight line,
those destinations far to the east and exotic. Every day
my father vanishes with his skilled hands,
with the seeds of his sweat, with his sleepiness,
and reappears at dusk and takes his meals
with us—his wife, his daughter, his angry son—
while all night long the planes grind upward.
We must hear them sometimes,
far aloft and rumbling. We lie awake
and dream our thoughts skyward—luck,
refusal, fear, and rage—and believe
now and then they get through, like prayers.
We are alone with ourselves,
our house a small darkness in the greater dark,
from which we might wave our hands bloody
and never be seen.

Simple Numbers

We knew nothing of women but spoke of them
in the bluntest particulars, the one girl
there giggling, drawing hard on
the reefer in her hand. In that whirl
of smoke and music, the ceremony we'd gathered for
was simple numbers: a calendar unstrung
across the wall, pictures of the war
clipped from magazines, eleven young
men and a younger girl, her eyes
dull with dope and abandon. Three of us lost that day,
and two of us, if what the tv said wasn't lies,
would be drafted, would take orders, would obey.

Take a boy's few years
in a man's husk, fill him with dying, and set him on
himself in another color, another country, another
world. Three of us lost, and two of us
one by one left for the bedroom and found her there
curled in the covers. Maybe we caressed
her, maybe we touched her in some gentle way for
a moment, and maybe felt in that moment
the blind beginnings of regret, before the smoke-buzz
and beer, the numbers, sent
us on her in the wrong equation we called love.

We believed in nothing but the abacus of hands,
the wealth of muscle, the drum
of our marching hearts, that intoxicating dance
in the problem of numbers, of which we ourselves were the sum.

Invisible Men

I

For the mile past American Steel
I breathed in my cargo of roses,
but even in that sweetness I could feel
the lung grit and chronic bloody noses
of my childhood. It was my last day
delivering flowers, and the dead man
these were meant to honor couldn't stay
dead in the town he lived in,
where the undertakers all were white.
Like me, doing my buck-an-hour duty,
driving deep into Venice, Illinois, and its blighted
air with a perfect spray of American Beauty
roses, Boston fern, and baby's breath for the casket.
What did I know? I was nineteen, a week
away from the army, and if you'd asked
I'd have just said, "Luck, bad luck,"
and looked away, believing for the moment in flowers.
I don't remember. Maybe I was told
it was all cosmetic, that even after hours
of trying, of dabbing at dead skin as cold
as any, no white man could make a black face
presentable. Maybe I believed that
the way I believed I'd go anyplace
the army sent me, the way I believed what
we'd all been told—dominoes and honor,
fine and fitting things, the old lies.
How could I have known any different? Conned or
gullible, probably both, I honed my eyes
on beer and smoke, my ears ringing
with wild guitars. In Venice that day,
late winter, young black men gathered singing
around trash-can fires, and no one looked my way.

A white boy with a job, a longhair,
I couldn't outshine the package store lights.
I was out of focus in the noxious air,
in March, when not even clouds were white.

2

What is that smell in funeral homes?
formaldehyde? ammonia? Chrysanthemums,
gladiolas, carnations, the roses I followed,
held out before me and nodding like beggars,
like mourners—*amen, amen,* my steps
murmuring down the carpeted hall. They were
gathered in the chapel, the family I slipped
past, though I felt them watch
while I nestled the casket-piece in place.
Flag-draped and sealed, steel-cold to the touch,
the coffin held a soldier, whose black face
grinned at me from an 8 x 10 portrait.
And what I don't understand today
is how I looked back at him without
so much as a blink, how I eased away,
cool and professional, slowly, making sure
the roses were right, balanced and symmetrical,
how, until I turned toward where
the family waited, I could not tell
they were crying. Silent, emptied, they
didn't look at me at all as I left,
but at one another, or at the plush gray
floor, or at the roses and fern and baby's breath—
expensive, short-lived, and meager. In that air
so full with dying, I moved like a wrist,
like sleep, impossible, invisible, there
and not there, like the people I passed
on the smoke-killed streets of Venice,
like the dead man I looked at but didn't see,

like the country itself imagining a menace
from across the world, while back home we
trucked our darker dead away and paid
ourselves little more than nothing to buy it:
the lie, the dazzling flag, frayed
to the edge of its true colors, white on white on white.

C.O.

We left the quarter peep shows, the lurid skin
magazines and comical, unimaginable toys,
and headed down the block toward the Quakers, a fever in
us from freedom and fear, a pure joy
our first trip away from the army in weeks.
They were American Friends, in a cluttered,
postered storefront, and the fleshy peeks
we'd taken left us shamed and flustered
before their devotion. Out the fly-specked window
and across the street the Alamo hunkered in dust
behind its gate. Our counselors knew the C.O.
route, would mention Canada only if they must,
and showed in their eyes a faith I
imagined as big as Texas. I could just make out
my face reflected in the window, about to cry,
a kid who knew only that he wanted out.

First they told us the rules: you must oppose
all wars and make no distinction between
them. No matter what violence goes
on around you, you must remain passive. Even
if your father is attacked by thugs, you
must say you'd only place your quiet, beatific self
between him and their blows. This is all you can do.
Here the counselors stopped, took from the shelf
the book of regs, and read the army's loaded
catechism, and we nodded and they went on.
But maybe then we daydreamed. Already a code
our fathers knew, and the country, was broken.
I was nineteen years old and could not tell
if I was a coward or a man of conviction,
didn't know if what I feared was a private hell
or the throes of our lovely, miserable nation.

And this is the simple end:
I pleaded the Christianity I've never believed
and got myself out. My American Friend
was a lawyer who drove a Mercedes and grieved
into tears each week at the list of the dead.
There was no sense in anything. And on the day
I got out, I went with Padilla, the Puerto Rican head,
to the quartermaster for paperwork and pay.
Padilla, from New York, beautiful and muscular
and younger than me. We smoked dope
and I woke up chilled, clammy with fear
before the last sergeant of my life. "I hope
you're glad," he said, and I was too high
and frightened to know what he really meant,
but he stamped my papers, paid me, and said good-bye,
then I found Padilla, and we shook hands, and went.

What My Father Believed

Man of his age, he believed in the things
built by men, the miracles of rockets and bombs,
of dams and foundries, the mind-killing
efficiency of assembly lines. And now the boredom
and blankness with which these students respond
to the tale of my father's loss of faith sadden me,
as times before I have saddened myself. Around
the middle of his life, I baited him wildly,
hung in my room the poster of Malcolm X,
whose lips were stilled around a word
that could have been freedom, or fight, or fuck.
I remember the first time I heard
my father say it. We had argued and I thought
I'd won. It was the same awful subject,
the war. I see now it was never how he had fought,
but his countrymen. He said we should not expect
to love war, but to know sometimes there was no way
around it, and I laughed and said,"Just stop."
In his eyes I saw what he couldn't say,
though right as I was, I could not
predict what he muttered. The rage that made
him flush and stutter and sweat was gone,
and only a fool of twenty couldn't see the blade
of pain he suffered, and suffered all along.
What should I say to him today, when the truth
I was so eager to embrace is constantly told,
when the plainness of it rankles like a bad tooth
in our mouths and the students scold
us both as naive and thoughtless. What of Custer?
they ask. What of racism? slavery? the inexorable theft
of every acre of native land? And I can muster
no answer they'll accept, but am left

at the end of class the argument's dull loser,
silent, contemplating the nature of instruction.
My father believed in the nation, I in my father,
a man of whom those students have not the slighest notion.

The Overcoat

The winter sun blinded, glass buildings
repeated the sky and all the endless traffic
trailed plumes of exhaust, white and vanishing.
I'd come out of the store wearing my new coat,
the old one in a box beneath my arm,
when I felt a hand on me.
He was old and white-haired. "I'll pay
you," he said. "I've got furniture to move.
I can't do it myself." Around us
the topcoated businessmen flew about
like leaves and pigeons strutted in the gutters.

I followed him south and east,
out of the glittery district of mirrors,
toward the fleabag hotels by the licorice factory.
The air was camphorous, our breaths flagged out
and sailed away. From a street of dead cars
he led me into a hall, smoke-dark
and redolent of licorice and urine.
Could I really not have known
what he wanted, there in the cold
and filth of that empty room,
when he turned to me and said nothing
but knelt as though to beg, his spotted hands
shivering? In that world unmade of glass
where the sun cannot shine, I knew. In that street,
that building, that brutal hall,
that room in which I gave away
what I had no need for.

The Grandmothers

He thought, this is the way they all are,
the grandmothers, and time is a cancer
we laugh through. He lit her cigarette
and handed it to her over the untouched hospital tray.
Her smile then, her perfect teeth—
they remained while the doctors whittled her away.

Single-lunged and breastless, diabetic and half-blind,
she ruled her house without rules.
Everywhere the heaped junk harbored its rats,
his parents feared tetanus and complained
about the sugar bowl, spoonfully eaten
in the late night tv's blue, blue glow.

One school night she wakened him,
hauled him groggy through rooms of sleep,
through the sleeping rooms, to the back porch,
that blistered ruin, and showed him
the distant storm, lightning's true skewers
and time-lapse thunder, the breeze rich with ozone.

On another, they left the house
carrying his books, his sacked, sweet lunch,
and walked the easy miles to the river,
where they swam utterly naked
and dug for mussels and slept on the beach
all the long night, then walked to school.

Even now, sand in his shoe brings her back,
or the tumble of the clothes dryer
she once let him ride. Lightning too,
and sugar, the wet-rot scent of rivers
and lakes, the moon-shiny swirl in a mussel's shell,
teeth and laughter, a cigarette's undulant smoke.

He thought, now she will die, and watched
the flame ooze slowly down the shaft.
Smoke curled out the tube between her ribs,
and with her free hand she gestured to it,
smiling. He thought, ozone, the ancient air,
the long, long night they must swim through.

for Les Barnes

Of Diamonds

The dew has sown a field of diamonds
behind his house. He warms his hands
on a coffee cup, scans the trails
of deer and elk back into the hills.
Though it is hunting season, they feed
on spent tomatoes in the garden, raid
the high grass of his fencerows.
Some even have come to the house, roses
below a bedroom window cropped away.
He has killed them in the past. Yesterday
the rifle sighted perfectly in, he swore
he'd be ready for half-light, the poor
straggling bull or buck easing off at dawn—
and he was ready, his rifle braced on
a banister, the elegant cross hairs
aligning, dividing the four quarters
of the heart. But something stopped him, kept
his finger still while the world slept
and the deer, oblivious as dew, stood,
then drifted out of sight to the woods.

Now, mid-morning, he is alone
and wondering. The children have gone
to school, his wife—a teacher—to her classes,
and as he watches a hawk pass
over the stubbled furrows, he feels
an overwhelming calm and ease. He will
survive all the seasons he can imagine,
his children will prosper, and the young men
who yearly fall in love with his wife
will know nothing of pain at his expense. If
they dream of her, he will understand.

They are like the deer and elk, walking the land
as though they were invisible, driven
by a hunger they cannot comprehend.
He lives his nights, and theirs
too, breathing in the air
from beloved sleepers, while the earth
is walked by animals unaware of the true worth
of diamonds.

Flight

All morning I have watched the robins
in their courtship flights and dances,
and I admit—before I thought
to come back to bed, to enter again
the orbit of your body
around sleep and dream—

that I thought at first of that man
you know and spoke of last night, a brilliant man,
a scholar, a sinecured and professional thinker,
who did not know and could not believe
there are men and women
who take the Bible as absolute fact.

"Even Jonah?" he asked. "Moses and the Red Sea?"
And he could not understand, and vowed,
you thought, silently, to remain
in all things skeptical, believing nothing
but the dreams of language, the sleep
that is the world we wake to.

What would he have seen in those robins?
What song in their raucous
clacks and jabbers? I believe in
a literal seduction, how undressed of flight
and feathers, that dance
is a language as keen as our own.

I believe when I came to you in your sleep,
when I was long awake, when I roused you half into
the world the robins weave their flights in,

that we too were literally aloft, that I licked awake
the wings from your shoulders, and we turned
and slanted and coasted down the same long breezes

as any birds, swallowed by the air, and believing.

In the Dark Pool, Finding You

No lights, no moon, no stars in the mountains,
clouds clearing the night with blackness and an owl
fooling from the pine at the edge of the meadow.
Lover, I am silent in these simmering waters,
the sulphur clouds we breathe are invisible
where you taunted me with nakedness
and swam away in tease. I am blind.

From his low bough bellows the owl, who
sees you, pink in the earth-cooked pool. I would have
eyes like his if I were dreaming, and a voice
to stir the night with, calling *where? where?*
Instead I am a muskrat, my mop of dark hair
wakelessly moving alleys over the surface
toward where I will find you and gently gnaw

your shoulder, where your skin will nearly squeak.
These are womb-waters, I say aloud, and the owl
goes quiet. I say I am a seed for you,
hoping you'll giggle, hoping somehow the water will
quicken and I'll know what corner you hide in,
what loop you swim around me, what vague dream
the eyes concoct in the lead an owl can live in.

Light is a trick of luck the blind man learns
to live without. Lover, here are my hands
imagining you, all swells and softnesses lightly giving.
In these waters, body-warm, I can make up
where you are, and it will be true.
This is love's skill and power, as real as the owl,
high in the pine, and dining on imaginary mice.

Onions

A rooster pheasant crows in the gully
out back, calls his hens, and they file
uneasily beneath the fence, across
the garden, and into the thicket
of star thistle and sage. The cat can't believe
his luck, stalks, then stalls at the sheer
numbers—twelve, sixteen, twenty-one
nervous, low-walking birds—there, everywhere,
then gone. I am on the porch
braiding onions, turning them,
rubbing them up like baseballs,
and the skins fall at my feet in a fluttery pile.
Every tree is losing its leaves, a dry
and skeletal snow, and the horse chestnuts fall
like bombs. The yard is rumpled with buckeyes.
Because it is autumn, because she is pregnant,
due, weary in her bones, beautiful
but feeling frumpy, my wife sleeps
in the living room, inside the heartbeat strike
of the pendulum clock, and dreams
she is making a baby from scratch,
a nubbin of flesh, a sphere around it—bone-colored,
translucent—then another, and another, shaped by her
hands, while outside all the air is
flushed with the scent of onions,
and the strands, a dozen each, hang
from the eaves of the porch until I move them
to the cellar, where they will remain for months.

A Memory of Garlic

Across the pale gray otherworldly umbras
shed by lights in the hospital parking lot,
over the lemony chevrons of pavement stripes
and into the shaded apartment house entry
as gold as the heart of a squash,
along the creaking sepia corridor,
a banister rising above us
and number 2-B aglow in the distance,
we are drawn by the aura of garlic.

For in a drift of papery husks
our friend has labored all afternoon,
until the bowl before him filled
as though with popcorn, that he might take
cool hand- after handful and unload them—
the moon slivers and ghostly shadows
of river-polished rocks—fifty cloves each
in four emptied birds, to simmer and stew
in the sweet, eye-watering, oven darkness.

And though you are pregnant, you enter
willingly into this autumn feast—a little
brown rice tinctured by soy, the year's last
barely turned tomatoes, and the camphorous flesh
of garlic-seething chickens. Out of the carcasses
the cloves tumble like half-formed eggs,
silvered, approaching translucence, butter-soft
and mild as this perfect September night.
He and I scoop them from the platter, and we eat.

Later, when we have said our goodbyes and lingered,
because this feast of garlic is our last,
because in a week our friend will leave—

as he must—when we have swum
from that current of richness and scent,
when I have become because of this meal
his magical twin, and he has become mine,
and the soul of this night unravels into other smells,
each one isolate and fading, our homeward steps

past parking lot lights grown huge as moons,
then you will take my hand and stop me
and we will embrace in some dark side street,
your belly swollen with its egg of new skin,
the wind all around us miserably clear
but your hair an airy cloud of garlic,
and my stunned, redolent body
a furnace from within, so many days smoldering
then flaring in a quarter moon's clove of smoke.

for Robert Johnson

Ravens at Deer Creek

Something's dead in that stand of fir
one ridge over. Ravens circle and swoop
above the trees, while others
swirl up from below, like paper scraps
blackened in a fire. In the mountains
in winter, it's true: death is a joyful flame,
those caws and cartwheels pure celebration.
It is a long, snowy mile I've come
to see this, thanks to dumb luck or grace.
I meant only a hard ski through powder,
my pulse in my ears, and sweat, the pace
like a mainspring, my breath louder and louder
until I stopped, body an engine
ticking to be cool. And now the birds.
I watch them and think, maybe I have seen
these very ones, speaking without words,
clear-eyed and clerical, ironic, peering in at me
from the berm of snow outside my window,
where I sprinkled a few crumbs of bread. We
are neighbors in the neighborhood of silence.
They've accepted my crumbs, and when the fire was hot
and smokeless huddled in ranks against
the cold at the top of the chimney. And they're not
without gratitude. Though I'm clearly visible
to them now, they swirl on and sing,
and if, in the early dusk, I should fall
on my way back home and—injured, weeping—
rail against the stars and the frigid night
and crawl a while on my hopeless way
then stop, numb, easing into the darkening white
like a candle, I know they'll stay

with me, keeping watch, moving limb to limb,
angels down Jacob's ladder, wise
to the moon, and waiting for me, simple as sin,
that they may know the delicacy of my eyes.

The Big Dipper

It is winter, we are driving at night,
my young son and I, when he sees
the first constellation of his life,
sees it really, clearly, peering
into the northerly sky over the emptiness
of central Idaho, the road glazed
along the river, the river star-washed, vivid
with its own constellations of rapid and wave,
sees it before I do, too keen
on the deadly highway, the subzero winds,
the arctic darkness hauled down by stars,
sees it and calls out its shape—
"like a big spoon, and there's its handle"—
and I know that I have told him before,
knelt behind him and pointed past his shoulder
to the bail that is a bear, delicate rust-ridden
dipper leaking star- and moonlight on us,
which he sees as well, and feels
grown-up about—this little knowledge
of the infinite I smile to understand,
seeing in his innocence and wonder my own,
which I hold out to him as though it were something
he might guide his life by, as though beyond
this treacherous, iced-over highway
there existed something I was bright enough to follow
on the long drive to where
we're headed, toward home, that cold house
dusted under hoarfrost, under the North Star.

Body and Soul

Yellow with newness, the other saxophones
throw rings of light across the auditorium ceiling,
but the brass of my son's horn has richened
to melted butter, an inch-deep translucence
on a bell of gold. I am straining to hear
his note among the many, the melody
rising out of flatness, the tempo lost
among the clatter of young tapping feet.

It looked decrepit at first, here and there
the chrome keys showing a dingy, plumber's brass,
two buttons emptied of mother of pearl.
But the horn man fixed all that:
polish and pearly disks and most of all
the way he breathed it into life
that day we picked it up.
From dozens of great, cloth-covered hooks
hung an orchestra of silence,
saxophones of every pitch and size,
the ungainly trombones and sinewy trumpets.
He sat on a padded barstool and played
"Body and Soul," slow and blue as night,
breath-soft but truly singing
in the bell of every idle horn.

Through the eastern window, sun shone
on his torch, his precision tools,
the floor all around him a litter of felt
and metal shavings, the stilled splashes of solder.
It was cathedral light and nightclub music
when he finished and spoke to my son
of his favorite players—Parker and Pepper,

their true hearts and perfect lungs
exchanging the night air with angels.

*

Neither of us speaks on the way home,
but in the middle of the living-room floor
he swabs his horn and reshines it,
nestles it in its battered brown case,
and looks. He points to a key, pokes it twice,
and says, "This is one the horn man fixed."
He pokes it again and again
and suddenly I know what he's thinking.
That tune the horn man played
wasn't a song at all, but something magic.
The way it swirled in the empty bells
had less to do with breath than wind,
the sort of wind that never wakes you
but brings some dream, in the scent
of flowers or the newly chilled air,
that for all your life you'll never forget.

The truth is, I'll be surprised
if music is his dream. For the moment
it's his mild affliction. He borrows Art Pepper
from my pile of tapes, and I hear moments later
the first plaintive notes of "Body and Soul."
It's late, he's a boy in a small American town
in love with believing, and despite anything
I might say, believes he's alone in the world.

Under the Double Eagle

                                        his pansies drink
the darkness down, replenishing their purples.
It is a country tune, fit for clogging,
for hobnobbing with a jug of shine,
neither lovely nor mournful, but the wind is
in a minor key, and the sliver of moon
behind the house fails to lighten where we are.
Faintly, his cigarette glows a slow
exaggerated pulse. It never leaves his mouth.
He has four daughters, all lovely, all newly women.
Out front the youngest one giggles and squirms
away from the boy who would touch her, but not so far
he can't. Back here, her father's reached
that part of the song where the tempo leans
foward into recklessness, and even though it's dark
I can feel his concentration, his care, I can sense
his willingness to let the tune take him
into that kingdom of blind men and saints,
wounded gawkers at stars, moon-stunned children
wild in bodies they entirely are feeling.
Now the wind picks up, now the tempo.
The ember of his cigarette brightens
until I can almost make out his face,
but not his hands, working above the supple strings,
making the guitar—from its elegant, rich-
scented chamber, its smooth grain and slim-waisted body—sing.

Parking

Today I live where I have always been
an adult, where I have always kept the same
job, known the same friends, driven
the same streets. What is it
that is not in me now, that has not been
in me for many years, that rigid
sense of direction that led me
always to where they were parked,
the coupled cars, bumper to bumper,
or side by side, windows glazed,
sweat-ridden, sodden with fumbling
and passion.
              Where are they?
Here, in the empty West, are they lost
so easily, so easily vanished into forests,
arroyos, the blind rutted ranch roads
to nowhere? Or were we—miners'
children, blessed in beer and whiskey, salted
early by the salty tongues of grandmothers—
allowed a wilderness our earth
could no longer afford? The times,
have they just got used to it all,
the motel lots each Saturday night filling
with jalopies.
              I would not trade
the familiar bedroom, the creak of spring,
the ease of middle age. But
somewhere I want to believe
the cars still rumble into place,
those hot rods, the lucky ramblers
in the station wagons of their fathers.
I want to believe the teeth still chatter,

from winter cold or summer passion.
I want to believe in an ardor as keen
as the homing pigeon's, who reconnoiters, banks,
lands, and coos like a fool in the dark.

Dust

From the hard-rutted, high-line road, the dust
billowed up like spindrift behind us,
a skin-colored cloud slowly ghosting away.
I loved the dry poultice a single summer day
could be in the mountains, even these mountains,
heavily timbered and ripped again and again
for their logs. I loved the dust as fine
as flour, settled in wind rows and sometimes—
in a low, exposed spot on a south-facing slope—
drifted over the road like a waterless pool, a swamp
of bones and dead men's breath, untracked
and hot as fresh ash. And it is a fact
that we usually exploded into such places
like children, laughing, while the dust chased
us along the road. But there was one
dry wash we stopped for: lake-sized, the pure dun
from moth wings troweled smooth as glass.
It was a miracle we waded into past
our knees, a hot bath of earth you swore
we could swim through, so we did, and it poured
into us like sun, like music, and we rose
on that other shore changed, our clothes,
our hair, our hands, our lips altogether earth.
That day, we learned again the easy worth
of motion, the truck a dead sea away,
idling, shimmery with heat, and in every way
the antithesis of mountains, their imperceptible dance,
their purity of waiting, those certainties we see as chance.

Steelhead

Salt-dazed in fresh water, he eats
nothing but the miles upstream, lame
ladders over dams and the silty back-
waters behind them, slack, brackish, and dull.

Some believe in the hatchery, some
in the river, but each believes in the code
for home. He makes his way shimmering,
all iridescence and muscle, a fog-bound apple

in the uphill world. His convex eye
beholds us, our emissaries of feather and steel,
and he strikes—no reason but the hell
of distance, the cantankerous, tiresome way.

If we are lucky, we love enough
to let him go. Unhooked, lightly held
near the surface of a pool, he'll sway
and pulse, drift and flex.

And in our numb fingers we'll feel him
come alive, the coil and re-coil
of heart and hard flesh, the slick shot snaked
toward oblivion, that pure dream of home.

                    —*in memory of Richard Hugo*

The White Cat

1

He swore this once he'd believe in magic,
that over miles and the crackling neurons of air
he'd know the instant his father died.
Under the same moon they were
constantly in touch—a chill in the August sun,
the white telepathy of snow: he would know,
he would know . . .
                    The earth itself
might show it, willows nodding, the hue
of late sun in a sagebrush gully.
I will taste his absence, he said, in water
or whiskey, smell it on the neck
of the newborn child. I will know.

2

That night he couldn't decipher the dream,
there was nothing, only darkness and his name,
its childish diminutive, hung in the air
like smoke. Had he heard it at all, rasped
once, or just the neighbors' rusty gate
swung wide in a wind?
                    He rose, walked
to the window, and listened. Streetlights
flickered through leaves, a white cat
padded down his driveway and stopped.
There was something in the bushes it saw,
and now it waited, still as stone.
Still as a root, it waited.

Night Calls

Locusts

No explanation will suffice, no dictionary
description nor entomological chart. Nothing
can keep him from dreaming the night's blue mouth,
the swirl, the rowel of locusts inside.
He awakens, eases up the sash closed earlier
against the noise, presses his boy's soft cheek
to the screen's crosshatch and rust, and listens.
His lips begin to form the syllable,
the round wow and whine of locusts—
dream-breath of all the empty world
he lives in, and speaks to, and loves.

The Midnight Whistle

On the drive across town he hears it.
He moves his one hand easily over the wheel,
with the other pulls the girl closer,
and she curls against his shoulder and side:
now the night possesses a little magic.
On the radio a DJ's voice drops
toward hot oil and smoke, the thrum
from the car's engine is power he controls.
He drives toward the country, the girl's
house and restless father, amazed
how after midnight, at fifty miles per hour,
the locusts still are a constant collective voice,
though now he can hear every mile
of the way a single blare louder than the others.

His Wife

At the edge of sleep, in the wash of the covers
he hears it, her sigh—half breath, half song—
and he is awake. For how long does he wait
on the far side of their bed? Minutes? Hours?
Then something pulls him on, the moon,
the memory of years before, in the half-dark
of his old car, her eyes moving him at will,
and he slides across the bed, magically
glides there as softly as the flow
of honey. Then he is against her,
holding her, easing her from sleep
as carefully as once he held her face in his hands
in the front seat of his car, and drew from her
that song of breath, that sigh he will always know.

His Children

In his dream it is the ruined farm
windmill, or his daughter, the little girl's breath
in sickness laborious and wet. He rises
to see and follows his hands through the darkness.
At the far end of the hall, the girl's room
bronzed from the pumpkin night-light,
thick with a vaporizer's fog. Next door
the older brother behind his lock and sneer,
dreaming impossible women. And there,
in the hallway of his mortgaged house,
in the narrow place where they all meet
and pass—his wife, his children, his local
unlistening self—he lies down to sleep
and hear. On one side the bruising silence,
on the other the tiny and regular rasps,
and the damp wind blowing into the hall,
making nothing better.

His Heart

Not insomnia, but the body's noisy sleep.
First he is aware of his breathing, that it is
something he must address—
like a pull-up bar, his hands white with rosin.
And when he rolls onto his back,
folds his hands across his chest, his heart
is marching there, muscling the dull limbs
and weary brain hard toward tomorrow.
He looks into the air above him: nothing.
He listens for any sign from the outside
world, any call but the code
his life is measured by, the rhythm
he dances to, that monotonous thump
he curses and yearns for.

The Scar

In her backpack the baby sputters and cheers
because I'm sitting on the sloped, grassy shore,
because her feet touch the ground. She pushes hard,
we rock. Her older brother flings bread
to the ducks on the pond, the few geese
honk and glower. It is days like these—
deep into autumn but warm as July,
the easy breezes and perfect sky
everywhere around us—when I almost believe
the world can be healed. And maybe it's the waves
from the paddling ducks that bring
the gunnysack of drowned cats rising
to the surface like a dream.
Maybe it's not cats at all, just some
fool's load of trash foolishly tossed here.
But the ducks give it a wide berth, and now they're
moving away, though my son keeps flinging
bread and the baby goes on jabbering
and the open weave of the burlap gradually breaks
the surface, and when it does the stench takes
the wind away and the sun shines
on our leaving, the sun in its blue dome,
the dying sun and a jet plane
leaving its smoke-like scar
silver in the autumn light, far, far
above our leaving, that scar, there,
unraveling already in cold, pure air.

Shrapnel

"Shrapnel," he says to me, "seems wrong,"
for the filament of steel that tore his spine
is nothing like what the word suggests.
Tiny, elegant, almost blunt,
it is his amulet in a film can,
each day taken out and caressed,
worn smooth and shiny as a bearing.

I have come to know him
through our morning walks, mine afoot,
his in a wheelchair with a shepherd dog
called Hue. Just as you probably suspect
he wears an army field jacket and a beard.
With an old racket he hammers a tennis ball
half a block for his dog to chase.

For a year now it is I
who have hit the ball for Hue,
while his master visits the naturopath
for herbal packs and high colonics,
his legs, he swears, more alive than ever,
shimmering in his lap with cold fire,
a sweet and unlocalized tingling.

He has asked me, politely, almost shyly,
for poems, and I give them to him—
Wilfred Owen and Weigl—
and he reads them on the spot,
slowly and carefully, like love letters
or contracts. Always, when he is finished,
he murmurs and folds them away in a pocket.

Sometimes we talk about the weather
or women, and then I have to leave
for school, so we wave and go our opposite ways,
he with his dog who loves him
and I with my messages of art
and the word. From the back porch
of his little house he watches

high school boys batter themselves silly
on the practice football field,
and I enter this new brick building,
stiflingly hot, ragged with conversations,
and stride to the front of the room
and survey the young faces, already bored,
and find, for some reason, I cannot speak.

I don't blame them, you know..
It must look those mornings
as though I've lost my mind, or my way.
I want to tell them sometimes I died
in the war I refused to go near.
Truly, I am ashamed
for my life, my lies, my legs.

Today, we will speak of Robert Frost,
his ambitions, his perfections.
They have read a few poems
and I have a film to show,
but as always I begin with a word,
something plucked from the blustery fall air
for no good reason but the mind

and its hard affiliations with the world.
I am quite entertaining some days,

going on about the harsh aesthetics of *phlegm*
or the mouthy succulence of *undulate.*
They know what's coming. I walk
back and forth, back and forth,
until the right word comes, and changes nothing.

Light after Light

1

Out of the corner of his eye it looked
like a carp, one of those gold-sided monsters
spinning in the shallows, a boil of scales and mud.
Or it was light, the sun a blonde scallop shimmering
over waves. He scanned the far shore and dreamed
another year, the nettles there and gnarled arms of thistles.
With two thousand other sailors he'd swept
hot dust the bomb test blew and basked
barefooted in the sweet Pacific sun.

And he knew the stillness well,
how smoke soothed his single lung and the miles
back to his junk-strewn shanty,
where the cool, bottled air remained.
One handed he'd rolled a joint, driven
the red clay Oklahoma back road to nowhere,
this cattailed, duckweedy slough.

In the light after light in the slant
toward dusk, he saw what it was and froze,
his hand spun limp off the slick-turning reel,
the wake of his line gone rippling through weeds.
She was blonde and bound in wire,
faceup and openmouthed. Already
the algae mottled her flesh.

2

Look at him, across his kitchen table.
He's barechested, a new growth lolls
below the scar on his ribs. His skin's
so leathery and dark the tattoos of his youth
barely show. What can you say to him here,

52

while the tv earsplittingly blathers and coffee boils
in a tin can on the stove?
                              That day he found her, when
he began to breathe again, the air was death-tinted,
but rich, a kind of humus in the wind. He turned,
broke his line, and left. He never said a word.

And now you're in it, that room
a dying man has come to, where the televised light flashes
on the little he owns: fishing tackle,
tools, sweet air in blue rented bottles.
And the light he watched one day
long ago was someone else's crime,
all the waters lit up and dying.

Finally, the tv's off, that Oklahoma heat
screws down. The story you've heard
lingers in the air like humidity
and the barking dogs of shantytown sound
musical as angels. You take a deep breath,
and out of the corner of your eye
see your own car, shiny and air-conditioned,
sleek for the long drive away.

—for Ruby York, atomic veteran

At the Vietnam Veterans Memorial

1987

In the sun and wet haze I am walking
a little north of west, my dark glasses wrong
for the icy finality of the place. No one's talking,
but a man in fatigues sings a quiet song
I can't remember, and I can't say why
I'm here. Like everyone else, to read
the names and finger the ones I knew, to cry
a little as I descend to the heart of the war. Perhaps I need
this pain. By the year I was drafted
refusals were common, a whole barracks of us waited
for word and could not believe the war had lasted
so long. We cursed, we thought we hated
everything about the land we'd learned at last to see.
And in the years since then, nothing has changed
my mind, nothing has made me
believe the lies or the truth rearranged
to suit a few men in charge. And what little I know
to be true is the names on this wedge of wall,
on the eastern brink of a nation that will not show
its blunders and murders and fools. I love all
these men, because they are dead,
because their deaths called out to me
warnings few among the living could have said,
and I believed them absolutely.
Should you go there, know this: that the walk
from the center of that wall is not the same
as any climb anywhere else. You walk,
but heavily, slowly, filled with the absent weight of names.

Camping

I see my father camping, twenty-seven years
ago grappling inside the canvas gullet of a tent
he made with Harvey Winkleman, in their spare time,
working lunches and breaks, sewing a shell
around a skeleton of coded tubing,
between parachutes and the fancified seats
of the personal planes of generals,
every day through winter and spring assembling
a camouflaged and round-shouldered pyramid
in which they would sleep with their families
for two fleeting weeks of summer vacation in Yellowstone
or the Ozarks, or alongside some newly made lake,
behind a dam, a smooth and miraculous monolith
made also by men, men like them,
who could imagine one flood controlling all others,
who could see themselves as well in the summers
upcoming, camping: the laughter of children
hiding in the woods or swimming in the shallows,
wives lying on the docks in the sun
or stirring some stew, squatting in the blue smoke
from the campfire.
              I see my father camping,
calling over twenty-seven years for one
then another and another of those numerically coded poles,
all twenty-eight of them, his voice rising
toward madness, the clink again and again
of the flashlight falling from his shaking hands,
the wild shaking of the canvas walls,
shaking of the pine boughs by the wind,
and my shivering mother and sister, still
in the car and huddled up front around the heater.
I see us speaking little over dinner,

cooked and eaten in the meager light
of the ancient Coleman lantern, the dinner instantly cold,
my mother shocked again by my father's temper,
my father raging toward fun, believing
like so many of his countrymen in that time
of blind prosperity, in the things
he could fashion with his hands and mind,
in the wisdom of what came down to him
from the ones he'd elected, from the ones
who'd won the war.
                              I see my father camping
today, still devoted in his way to manufacture
and technology. Carefully he backs his trailer into place,
carefully he cranks his jacks, eases
the bubble of his level toward center.
He is old, he says, and deserves these
comforts, but I do not believe him.
He has always deserved his life, like the rest of us,
and now he walks with my mother along the trails
in the woods, across the beaches, and they look
like lovers. We're warred out,
he says, and he means his country,
and his rages he confines to a muttered obscenity,
a shrug of disgust for what passes these days for wisdom.
Retired, he thinks of his occupation as camper,
listener, and he understands at last what brought him
out of town. We look at one another through the smoke
of the campfire. We do not speak.
It is the quiet he strains to hear,
the noisy silence of another world he has grown nearer to
this late in his life.
Listen, another day is almost gone.

The Wishing Tree

My son left his notebook on the picnic table
and took his rod and reel down
to the river to fish. A little breeze blew
the pages over, blew smoke my way
from the fire we had drunk our coffee and chocolate by.
I was washing the breakfast dishes,
enjoying my hands in the hot sudsy water
and the steam from them rising as I dried
metal plates and wooden spoons and laid
the iron skillet top down on a flat stone
by the fire. I even enjoyed just sitting there,
watching grouse blunder stupidly out of the brush
and into our campsite, enjoyed just looking
at the drawings and stories in my son's notebook—
the great trout and sheer unclimbable mountains, the sun
with its penicilled-in, symmetrical rays, the tales
about football and horses and school,
and an old Indian man who found a tree for wishes.

And now I wish I had stopped looking, and loafing,
wish I'd risen and wrestled on my waders.
I wish I'd left camp and seen my son at the river
hold up a lunker trout, gingerly, by the jaw—
the way I'd taught him. I wish
I'd tossed away my coffee and gone,
but I didn't. I stayed there, looking
at a thing he'd drawn, a picture of rockets,
rows of them, ranks and ranks of them
like the fences from suburban backyards
foreshortened by a telephoto lens,
and fire, everywhere flame and smoke,
ruins and rubble, everywhere
but a white sphere of peace, a circle at the bottom of the page,

in which two people played catch.
In their little space, they were all
out of proportion, as large as the rockets
that surrounded them, and their mouths
simple, straight, bold lines—not the usual smiles—
as though the game they played required the strictest concentration,
as though for some reason they could never
let the ball not be caught, as though everything
depended on them, everything—
and in the picture, it did, it did.

Poetry from Illinois

History Is Your Own Heartbeat
Michael S. Harper (1971)

The Foreclosure
Richard Emil Braun (1972)

The Scrawny Sonnets and
Other Narratives
Robert Bagg (1973)

The Creation Frame
Phyllis Thompson (1973)

To All Appearances: Poems New
and Selected
Josephine Miles (1974)

The Black Hawk Songs
Michael Borich (1975)

Nightmare Begins Responsibility
Michael S. Harper (1975)

The Wichita Poems
Michael Van Walleghen (1975)

Images of Kin: New and
Selected Poems
Michael S. Harper (1977)

Poems of the Two Worlds
Frederick Morgan (1977)

Cumberland Station
Dave Smith (1977)

Tracking
Virginia R. Terris (1977)

Riversongs
Michael Anania (1978)

On Earth as It Is
Dan Masterson (1978)

Coming to Terms
Josephine Miles (1979)

Death Mother and Other Poems
Frederick Morgan (1979)

Goshawk, Antelope
Dave Smith (1979)

Local Men
James Whitehead (1979)

Searching the Drowned Man
Sydney Lea (1980)

With Akhmatova at the Black Gates
Stephen Berg (1981)

Dream Flights
Dave Smith (1981)

More Trouble with the Obvious
Michael Van Walleghen (1981)

The American Book of the Dead
Jim Barnes (1982)

The Floating Candles
Sydney Lea (1982)

Northbook
Frederick Morgan (1982)

Collected Poems, 1930–83
Josephine Miles (1983)

The River Painter
Emily Grosholz (1984)

Healing Song for the Inner Ear
Michael S. Harper (1984)

The Passion of the
Right-Angled Man
T. R. Hummer (1984)

Dear John, Dear Coltrane
Michael S. Harper (1985)

Poems from the Sangamon
John Knoepfle (1985)

Eroding Witness
Nathaniel Mackey (1985)
National Poetry Series

In It
Stephen Berg (1986)

Palladium
Alice Fulton (1986)
National Poetry Series

The Ghosts of Who We Were
Phyllis Thompson (1986)

Moon in a Mason Jar
Robert Wrigley (1986)

Lower-Class Heresy
T. R. Hummer (1987)

Poems: New and Selected
Frederick Morgan (1987)

Cities in Motion
Sylvia Moss (1987)
National Poetry Series

Furnace Harbor: A Rhapsody
of the North Country
Philip D. Church (1988)

The Hand of God and a Few
Bright Flowers
William Olsen (1988)
National Poetry Series

Bad Girl, with Hawk
Nance Van Winckel (1988)

Blue Tango
Michael Van Walleghen (1989)

The Great Bird of Love
Paul Zimmer (1989)
National Poetry Series

Eden
Dennis Schmitz (1989)

Waiting for Poppa at the
Smithtown Diner
Peter Serchuk (1990)

Great Blue
Brendan Galvin (1990)

Stubborn
Roland Flint (1990)
National Poetry Series

What My Father Believed
Robert Wrigley (1991)